CALVIN COOLIDGE'S UNIQUE VERMONT INAUGURATION

The Facts Winnowed from the Chaff: the Authentic Account
of the Swearing in of Calvin Coolidge as 30th President
of the United States by his father at the Coolidge
Homestead, Plymouth Notch, Vermont in 1923.

by

VREST ORTON

D0815178

Published by
ACADEMY BOOKS
Rutland, Vermont

in Cooperation with
The Calvin Coolidge Memorial Foundation, Inc.

PREFACE TO THIRD EDITION

The decade following the restoration of the Birthplace was an eventful one for the National Historic District at Plymouth Notch. The entire focus of the original national Board of Trustees of the Calvin Coolidge Memorial Foundation had been directed toward the construction of a Visitor's Center to house a small museum, gift shop, lounge and restrooms, with parking facilities geared to the increasing trend of visitors and tour busses.

Through the foresight and generosity of the Eva Gebhard-Gourgaud Foundation, additional funding was obtained to provide the "snecked ashlar" construction of the stone masonry of the main building. The stones were drawn from the local quarry which provided material for other early Plymouth buildings. The roof is of Vermont slate.

An outstanding photographic essay of President Coolidge's life, with captions derived from his Autobiography, was created in the museum ell by William B. Pinney, Director of the Vermont Division for Historic Preservation.

A gala centennial celebration of the President's birth on July 4, 1972, culminated in the dedication of the Center.

The following year, on August third, another significant celebration was held to commemorate the fiftieth anniversary of the "homestead inauguration." Shortly thereafter, it became known that the President, having some qualms about the legality of his father's participation in his private ceremony, underwent a secret, second swearing-in by Supreme Court Justice A. A. Hoehling, shortly after his arrival in Washington.

ISBN 0-914960-31-8
Library of Congress No. 81-66760

Copyright © 1970 by
The Calvin Coolidge Memorial Foundation, Inc.
Printed in Vermont, U.S.A.

First Edition, 1960   Second Edition, 1970
Third Edition, 1981   Fourth Edition, 1998

PREFACE TO SECOND EDITION

This new edition published by The Calvin Coolidge Memorial Foundation (for an account of its aims see back cover) is, with minor changes, a facsimile of the first edition. The right to publish has been given by Mr. Orton, as a gift to The Foundation to assist its work at Plymouth.

Since 1960 when this book was first published, Mr. Orton reports that two persons have made public claims that they also were present at the inauguration of President Coolidge on the night of August 3, 1923. There is no foundation to these claims, Mr. Orton states, and further declares: "All who were present on this historic night, including Mrs. Calvin Coolidge, made statements to me before I wrote the book declaring the accuracy of my account. In 1966 and 1967, when these two claimants tried to carve a place for themselves in the Coolidge history, only three of those originally there were alive. These men were Joseph H. Fountain, then Mayor of St. Albans, Vermont, and Joseph McInerney and Herbert Thompson, both then retired. Not only did they declare that no other persons, except those named in this book, were present at the historic ceremony, but that they had never even heard of the new claimants.

Between the first (1960) and the second (1970) editions of this book several important changes have taken place at Plymouth Notch.

In 1968, through the Board of Historic Sites, the state acquired the General Store and Post Office. Restoration of the Presidential birthplace was commenced with the removal of a modern enclosed porch. Appearing in early photographs to be unpainted, this building back of the store is now a distinctive dark red in contrast to the community of white buildings.

The furnishings have been donated by the Coolidge family and many are those actually used by the President's parents in the birthplace.

DEDICATION

To My Wife

ELLEN

ABOVE: Mr. Coolidge at the Adams House, Boston, where he lived when a member of the Legislature and state Senator, taken on the day he received the news of his nomination as vice president of the United States.

I

THE LEGENDS AND THE HUMOR

PROLOGUE

This book is not offered as a defense of Calvin Coolidge or of Vermont although both have often been misunderstood by writers whose horizons are bounded by the cities in which they live.

There have been those who partially understood the 30th president of the United States—authors who wrote books and newspapermen who wrote articles. But in treating what seemed to be the high points of his career they failed to uncover all of the details about one event of three minutes duration that may, in the long perspective of history, prove to be the most dramatic and the longest remembered episode of all.

I refer, of course, to the night-time ceremony in a small village house in the remote hills of Vermont where, by the light of a kerosene lamp, Calvin Coolidge's father administered to his son the oath of office as president of the United States.

This story means a great deal to us Vermonters. That hundreds of thousands of Americans make the Plymouth pilgrimage to see the house where this event took place, confirms my faith that it also means a great deal to the people of the United States. I think therefore, that I need no excuse for trying to present the fullest possible account of this epochal event.

It seems to me that two points of view are necessary to understand the character of the 30th president of the United States; and that unless they are taken into account his place in history cannot be understood.

The first:—as of the folk heroes Sam Houston, Jim Bowie, Davy Crockett, Henry Ford and our own Vermonter, Ethan Allen, there is a constantly growing body of legends about Calvin Coolidge that seems more alive than the actual fact of history. These men actually lived in *history* but now they seem to live more vividly in legend. There is nothing wrong in this. Because it is so, they come alive in a fresh, new fashion to each generation of Americans . . . each generation adding lively embellishments of its own. These unique men have a special immortality that is denied many of the so-called "famous" men of history. I am sure that could any of these have had their way with posterity, they would have chosen to live in the tales of the American folk even at the expense of a more formal commemoration in marble or the printed word.

With this odd manifestation of fate, Calvin Coolidge would, I think, have been pleased. Even during his lifetime his sense of humor afforded him considerable satisfaction at having out-witted (if one may use that word) the more urban, sophisticated, distinguished and assuredly richer Coolidge clan of Boston and environs, not to omit Cambridge. The distinguished Coolidges of Boston are nobly embedded in the history . . . of Boston. The story is still told in Harvard yard of the alumnus who happened to be in Europe in 1923. The news that Coolidge had been made president of the United States hit him with a slight shock. He had never even heard that Archibald Cary Coolidge, Harvard Professor of European History, was running for that office!

The second phenomenon about Calvin Coolidge has to do with humor. There is a distinction between a sense of humor and dirty tricks. No one not born and bred in Vermont will want to understand this. But here it is . . . .

The humor of the Vermonter of which Mr. Coolidge was the classic exemplar is dry, like a wine of the Graves region. It is also frugal. No words are wasted in explanation. It is dramatic although unwittingly so. A Vermonter will relate a simple, innocent story which seems to have no point and is

concerned only with common daily happenings. While you are pondering, suddenly the point will hit you. This device is the sturdy basis of all great comedy since the days of the Greeks. Lastly some Vermont humor may seem like a trick, often known as a practical joke, but it is never a dirty trick that hurts people or leaves a sour, bitter taste.

＊1

Let me illustrate this observation with two Coolidge stories. One day a new congressman called on the President. As he finished the visit and stood up he said, "Mr. President, I wonder if you could give me something I could take home to show the folks just to prove I was talking to the President of the United States. I don't care what it is . . . just so long as it is something of yours. If I could have a band off one of your cigars, that would be fine."

President Coolidge reached into his desk, took a box of cigars and drew out one. Holding it between his forefinger and thumb, he deftly removed and handed to the Congressman one cigar band. The Congressman thanked him and left.

Later the story got around. One day Mr. Stearns, one of the few men on really intimate terms with Calvin Coolidge, asked the President about this.

"It it true," Mr. Stearns demanded in a bantering tone, "that you actually removed the band and handed *that* to the man?"

"Yes, it is." Mr. Coolidge replied.

"Well, I don't understand why you didn't give him the whole cigar."

The President, with a grin replied, "He only asked for the band."

This was the kind of acuity Mr. Coolidge enjoyed. It is an integral part of our traditional Vermont humor. First, because Vermonters are literal: they never think or talk in double meanings. Second and even more revealing, Vermonters don't like hinting. Having people ask them for a gift doesn't set well. But they had much rather have someone ask outright than to hint. Calvin Coolidge knew very well the Congressman really wanted the cigar. But since he didn't say so, it tickled the President to give him literally what he did ask for the band. Third, Mr. Coolidge liked this kind of mild joke. Many of his jokes followed the pattern of turning the tables on someone by doing what the other person least suspected. I therefore believe that this Coolidge story is authentic because it is true to the Coolidge character.

Now let's take the other story. It has been told and retold
but its essence is this—the night of the homespun inaugural at
Plymouth Notch, so the yarn goes, and a very fine yarn it is,
a number of men walked over to the village store with Mr.
Coolidge where he made a telephone call. After he put in the
call he then turned to the men and said, "Any of you want a
drink?" They all said they did. He stepped up to the counter
and told Florence Cilley, the storekeeper, to give each of them
a bottle of Moxie. He took one himself. Just as they were
finishing the drinks, the telephone rang. Mr. Coolidge arose,
took his empty bottle over and set it on the counter. Reaching
into his pocket he pulled out a nickel, laid it carefully down on
the counter and exclaimed, "Here's the pay for mine." Then
he went to answer the telephone.

Knowledge of Mr. Coolidge's character makes many of us
Vermonters feel that this story doesn't ring true. It just
doesn't seem the kind of thing Mr. Coolidge would have done.

He was frugal but not stingy. He was careful but not par-
simonious. He was laconic but not contumelious. He did not
deliberately set out to hurt other people's feelings. And further,
he didn't play dirty tricks. He liked to play a mild practical
joke but only when he could see the effect of it.

For example, the time his wife, Grace, purchased from a
door-to-door salesman a book on home remedies and left it on
the table for Calvin to see when he came home. Calvin saw it
and wrote these words on the flyleaf for Grace to see when she
came in. "I don't see any cure in here for suckers."

This was, I think, a typical Calvin Coolidge idea of
humor. But not paying for the drinks which he had himself
invited the men to take, was not. The Moxie story is a wonder-
ful story but somehow it seems just too good to be true!

Coolidge yarns could be cited *ad infinitum*[1]. One could line

[1]Even as late as 1959, one careless writer wrote a story of Calvin Coolidge in which not only were all the old unfounded tales repeated, but many
new ones concocted and offered as gospel truth.

up in one column those that sound true and in another those that seem fabrications or suspicious inventions of jokesmiths whose name, when it comes to folk-heroes like Coolidge, is legion. But to do this would be fruitless. Two suffice to make the point.

And my final point is this: that to understand and appreciate what I believe is the authentic story[1] of the homespun inaugural of Calvin Coolidge as President of the United States, at Plymouth Notch on August 3, 1923, it is essential to sense the difference between the native humor and under-statement natural to Vermont-born Calvin Coolidge and the fiction embroidered on the plain fabric of the man's life.

---

[1]Authentic, that is, as far as it is possible for one person, with no more then five years at his disposal to gather facts. There will always be, of course, conflicting accounts offered because it's human to enlarge on fact and rumor, as well as to forget what actually did happen. As a good example of this human failing to forget, and then to add embellishment to a story, one person in Plymouth told me that on the morning of August 3, 1923, this person decided to go to the Coolidge Homestead. Arriving, this person found Mrs. Calvin Coolidge seated in a rocking chair, on the porch, rocking away . . . at two o'clock in the morning! Mrs. Coolidge, so *this* yarn goes, jumped up and made the stranger welcome in time to witness her husband take the oath of office!

II

CALVIN COOLIDGE
AND THE STATE OF VERMONT

Beginning the next morning after Mr. Coolidge took the oath of office at Plymouth Notch, the people began to come. Many stood and silently gazed at the Coolidge house, many wanted to get in. As the years went by the crowds increased until during the summers from 1923 to the end of Coolidge's second term, this village home was surrounded.

There was nothing wrong with this: some of course were the idle and the curious, but most came because they had been intrigued and moved by the warm hearted and romantic story of what had taken place in this house on August 3, 1923.[1]

No, there was nothing wrong with the crowds . . . but there was something decidedly wrong with the entrepreneurs who figured they could make some fast money out of the crowds. In a short time, the lawns in front of the church across the road, and even the road itself were dotted by hucksters selling things. The local store was expanded to give more room for enterprising and profitable concessionaires. The scene soon resembled the dusty, scuffed-up atmosphere of a carnival or of some outworn European shrine.

There were always a number of amusing aspects to this scene. I remember so well, visiting the carnival one hot summer when Mr. Coolidge was in residence. Ensconced directly

---

[1]Edward Whiting was to say, a year later, "If I could make ten million men go through the town of Plymouth, I would have ten million votes for Calvin Coolidge. He is like his country and his country is the essential soul of America."

across the road within perhaps 50 feet of where the President sat on his own front porch trying to entertain his friends such as Henry Ford, Thomas Edison and John Burroughs, sat a curious figure. This was a roly-poly little fat man trying to make a living. He sat on a folding chair and on a folding card table he displayed his curious wares. I have somewhere in my collection a snapshot in which the photographer caught both the man at his table and one of the wandering hens directly under the table. The man's mouth and the hen's were both open:—the man was trying to sell a book.

His wares consisted of four or five brochures and one bound book. He had written them all. In the brochures were verses . . . in the book a story which I was never able to read, and I doubt if any person was. But I remember the title vividly: "The Axe with the Three Nicks." The proud author had, of course, paid some vanity publisher in Boston his hard earned savings for issuing this "literature" and now he was trying to get his money back.

He was one of many who were also trying to get their money back and perhaps a little more.

I remember thinking how incongruous it was for the President of the United States, one of the most powerful men in America, unable to do a thing about these annoyances because the fakirs had settled their stands on church property or in the road which was town property. Mr. Coolidge and his guests learned to pay no attention to all this. But in visiting with him and his charming wife during those years, I learned that had it not been for their extreme kindness and past experiences in steeling themselves for the ordeal of public attention, they might have expressed some polite demurers.

There were, however, an increasing number of disturbed persons who did express stronger sentiments than polite demurers. State officials from the Governor down received such protests. One of the most concerned was a Plymouth native, Herbert Moore. Herb, as he was known to thousands of visitors, had acted as unofficial greeter for years, attempting to make people feel at home in his village.[1] And to tell them about his cousin, Calvin.

Herbert Moore got himself elected to the Legislature especially to do something about Plymouth and urge this assembly to assume an obligation to the memory of Calvin Coolidge. The town apparently was helpless or unwilling to clean up the unseemly conditions in this tiny Vermont village where exploitation and rank commercialization dominated the rural scene. The State must act.

The State acted in the legislative session of 1947 by creating a Vermont Historic Sites Commission and enjoining this instrumentality of the state government to "pay especial attention to Plymouth" and the properties there associated with Calvin Coolidge.

Ever since that time this State Commission has been attempting to carry out the mandate of the Vermont General Assembly.

The first step was to call on Mrs. Coolidge who was then spending her summers in the Coolidge Homestead. Earle W. Newton, the first chairman of the Commission, accompanied by John Clement[2] went to Plymouth in August, 1947. Mrs. Coolidge had been receiving a large body of women. It was a hot, uncomfortable and very humid day. As these women left, Newton asked Miss Aurora Pierce, the housekeeper who was sitting on the porch, if he and Clement could see Mrs. Coolidge. "She's in there!" Miss Pierce said, pointing to a door leading into the new wing the President had built in 1932. As they entered and stepped down into the room, Mrs. Coolidge was seated in a chair. She looked tired and bedraggled. Newton exclaimed, "We're the Historic Sites Commission." Mrs. Coolidge looked up and smiled, wanly: "I guess I'm a historic sight myself!" she said.

---

[1]Herbert Moore was the father of Joe Moore, now representative of Plymouth in the Vermont Legislature and caretaker of the state owned Coolidge Homestead.

[2]Clement was a member of the Commission and in 1959 became President of the Vermont Historical Society.

The next step taken by the Commission was to acquire the Wilder house next door to the Coolidge homestead. This was one of the properties assuredly "associated with Calvin Coolidge" for in it, in 1846, his mother, Victoria Josephine Moor, had been born. After she married John Coolidge and went to live in the Coolidge home, her sister Gratia Moor, who had married a man named John Wilder, occupied the house. Thus it became known as the "Wilder house", although it was actually the Moor place.

By 1947 it had fallen into decay and was actually a ruin. To restore the neat, well kept appearance of the village that prevailed during Mr. Coolidge's boyhood, it was necessary to clean up this disgraceful eyesore.[1]

※ 4

The same moribund (no pun intended) condition prevailed in the Plymouth Notch Cemetery. This ancient burying ground, where all the Vermont generations of Calvin Coolidge's ancestors were buried and where rested now the President and his young son, Calvin Junior, who had died during Mr. Coolidge's presidency, was in deplorable condition. Stone walls had crumbled, erosion had pulled soil down the 45 degree slope into the road and coarse grass and bushes had grown up. In order to get near enough to see the gravestone of the President of the United States, one had to get over a stone wall and climb up a side-hill.

---

[1]It was unfortunate that in later years the Commission was unable to control the reconstruction of this building. It should have been restored to its original condition but instead, it was rebuilt by the Vermont Department of Forests and Parks according to their own ideas.

OPPOSITE: Entrance to Calvin Coolidge Homestead at Plymouth, showing the official marker of the Vermont Historic Sites Commission.

Obtaining the permission of the local Cemetery Association the Historic Sites Commission spent several thousand dollars in restoring this area. Dry laid stone walls were reset and repaired, a dry-laid stairway of stones was constructed so the public might walk up and actually see the President's grave, and the erosion of the steep side hill terrain was put to an end. The Cemetery Association, after national publicity in newspapers and magazines had called attention to the unkempt condition of the place, cut the grass and chopped down the bushes.[1]

---

[1]The Coolidge family, however, always took care of the Coolidge lot.

The other two major properties associated with the President were, of course, the Coolidge Homestead and the President's birthplace.

In 1872 when Calvin was born, his father owned and operated the small village store. In back of this building stood a plain, unpainted simple clapboard house, one-storey high, with window and door facing north. In a downstairs bedroom of this modest cottage Calvin was born on July 4, 1872. By this time his father had become a man of parts in southern Vermont.

One of the most versatile figures in the state, Colonel John Coolidge held many town and state offices, was Vermont agent for Dun and Bradstreet, and in fact undertook so many outside interests that he was soon obliged to devote himself wholly to these multitudinous affairs. Four years after Calvin's birth he gave up the store, bought the present homestead property across the road and moved into it. Here, of course, in addition to the new horsehair parlor set and piano purchased in Boston for his wife, he moved what were without doubt the sparse furnishings of that first household. Amongst these was the bed in which Calvin had been born and the other meager furniture of that small bedroom. This is why today these historic furnishings are in the state-owned Coolidge Homestead on public display.

The State of Vermont, however, was not so fortunate in "doing something" about the other property once associated with the President. This was the privately owned birthplace cottage. After the President's birth in 1872 it had been connected to the store and subsequently, by the addition of a side porch and raising the roof, incorporated into the store building.

BIRTHPLACE OF CALVIN COOLIDGE

This rare photograph of the President's birthplace is used with the permission of Mrs. Charles Hoskison, owner of the photograph.
clapboarded one-storey house, with shed attached, stood back of the present village store. Mr. Coolidge was born in the room at the left on July 4, 1872. Later this building was wholly changed and incorporated into the store building. When the President was born here, as this picture shows, it was not part of the store.

Many attempts to buy this property were made by the Vermont Historic Sites Commission. Other attempts were advanced to obtain cooperation so that the actual birthplace structure might be put back to its original condition of 1872 and restored to genuine authenticity by the Commission. Philanthropic individuals also attempted to buy the property in order to save it from commercial exploitation and restore it to public preservation and care. All these attempts failed. Today the individuals who own this structure are operating it as a private "historic site" according to their own notions of what is proper and fitting.

Mr. Coolidge on "Captain", the family all-purpose horse, in front of the Coolidge Homestead.

However, the most important site associated with President Coolidge was the undoubted Coolidge Homestead.

Here Calvin lived from the time he was four years old. From this village home he attended local school and later Black River Academy in Ludlow. During his years at Amherst College he came to this house for vacations. In after years, from the time he began his political career as Mayor of Northampton, Massachusetts, and on up through his offices of State Senator, Lieutenant Governor, Governor, and Vice President of the United States, this was the home he loved and this was where he brought his family when he could get away from his duties. Here his beautiful young sister, Abigail, died when she was thirteen. In the front room his equally beautiful mother, Victoria Josephine Coolidge, died in 1885. This home was a place hallowed in memory and strong in that moving sentiment toward his family that Calvin Coolidge expressed in almost poetic terms in his *Autobiography*.[1]

---

[1]Of Plymouth Notch, he wrote:

"It would be hard to imagine better surroundings for the development of a boy than those which I had. While a wider breadth of training and knowledge could have been presented to me, there was a daily contact with many new ideas, and the mind was given sufficient opportunity thoroughly to digest all that came to it.

"Country life does not always have breadth, but it has depth. It is neither artificial nor superficial, but is kept close to the realities.

"While I can think of many pleasures we did not have, and many niceties of culture with which we were unfamiliar, yet if I had the power to order my life anew I would not dare to change that period of it. If it did not afford me the best that there was, it abundantly provided the best that there was for me."

And of his mother he wrote:

"She was practically an invalid ever after I could remember her, but used what strength she had in lavish care upon me and my sister . . . There was a touch of mysticism and poetry in her nature which made her love to gaze at the purple sunsets and watch the evening stars. Whatever was grand and beautiful in form attracted her. It seemed as though the rich green tint of the foliage and the blossoms of the flowers came for her in the springtime, and in the autumn it was for her that the mountain sides were struck with crimson and with gold."

(22)

Dedication Ceremony July 1, 1957. John Coolidge, the President's son presenting the Coolidge Homestead to the state of Vermont. At left sits the then Lieut. Governor Robert T. Stafford of Vermont. Standing next to Mr. Coolidge is Vrest Orton. Behind him at right is Meade Alcorn, then chairman of the Republican National Committee and principle speaker at this ceremony. On the platform are representatives of the Governors of Mass., Rhode Island, Conn. and New Hampshire. Hidden behind the speaker is the then Governor of Vermont, Hon. Joseph B. Johnson.

※8

But the dramatic interest in the Coolidge Homestead centered, obviously, in the unique event which took place there on August 3, 1923.

These facts assuredly made the Coolidge Homestead the outstanding property in Plymouth Notch associated with President Coolidge and thus became the major objective of the Vermont Historic Sites Commission.

It was therefore a great source of pride that after several visits with John Coolidge, Calvin Coolidge's son who then lived in Farmington, Connecticut, I was able to make arrangements

(23)

so this historic edifice could come to the State of Vermont.[1] In 1956, the property having previously been deeded to John and his wife, Florence Trumbull Coolidge by John's mother, Grace Coolidge, they presented this magnificent gift to the State. It was accepted and dedicated in a public ceremony on August 3, 1957 by Governor Joseph B. Johnson and turned over to the Vermont Historic Sites Commission.

It then became my privilege to work out with the professional assistance of Payson Rex Webber, A. I. A., of Rutland, an access arrangement to all the rooms of the first floor.[2] By utilizing halls and corridors and glass partitions in front of doors, we were able to show the public each room of this simple Vermont house and to show each exactly as the way it looked on the night of August 3, 1923.

This was made possible by the generous gift of John Coolidge and his wife of all the furnishings, down to the last small pincushion on the bedroom bureau, that were in the house in 1923. In the pleasant task of arranging these furnishings I was assisted by Mrs. Kate Ward, and Mr. and Mrs. Charles Hoskinson who, as Plymouth neighbors, had known and visited this house many times.

However, to make sure we would place everything precisely where it had been on the night of August 3, 1923, I hesitated to trust memories. I soon found myself reading very carefully all that had been published about this historic event.

As this research deepened a very strange fact emerged.

The story that follows rests, in a manner of speaking, upon this strange fact.

---

[1]Up to June 10, 1959, when I resigned, I had served as a member of the Vermont Historic Sites Commission for ten years and as its Chairman for eight. During this decade I had discussed the state's interest in the Coolidge Homestead with Mrs. Calvin Coolidge. She felt that the State ought to acquire the birthplace property and as soon as this had been accomplished, she would donate the Homestead. Since, however, she later came to realize the impossibility of the state's obtaining the former, she decided just before her death in 1957 that it was time for us to acquire the latter.

[2]The State of Vermont is greatly indebted to Mr. Webber for his generous contribution.

This unique photograph of the President shows him in a humorous mood and with an expression seldom if ever caught by any other photographer. It was taken on a summer day at the Coolidge Homestead.

(25)

III

THE WOMAN WHO WASN'T THERE

On a sultry mid-summer's night thirty-seven years ago the muse of history touched briefly a remote hill village in Vermont and laid upon this sleeping hamlet of some twenty odd souls a unique distinction that forever lifted the time, the place and the house to a permanent niche in American annals.

The muse of history is fleeting.

The event that drew Plymouth Notch from dim obscurity into a national spotlight lasted only three minutes. Calvin Coolidge stood by a table in the front room of his Vermont home and repeated after his father, a Vermont notary public, the oath of office as president of the United States. It was 2:47 on the morning of August 3, 1923.

There are and always will be many shades of opinion about Mr. Coolidge as a president. No one, however, has disputed the uniqueness and the ineluctable drama of this starkly simple scene. Of the twenty-nine presidents before him, none had ever been inaugurated in his own home . . . none by his own father. The homemade ceremony itself and the curious steps that led to it, constitute one of the most appealing and

OPPOSITE: MISS AURORA PIERCE Shoveling Snow.

This unique photograph, taken by Mrs. Charles Hoskison and used with her permission, is the only picture showing Miss Pierce in the last years of her life. In this picture she is shovelling the deep snow in front of the Coolidge Homestead. It was not unusual to see snow drifts in front of this house almost head high, as this one is.

heartwarming stories in our history. School children will, I think, be reading it long after more startling segments of our past, heavy with pomp and circumstances have been forgotten. It is a story touched by the magic of legend and it has, over the years, taken on the starlight charm of an American folk tale.[1]

Yet, the muse of history is fickle.

Inaugurations of other presidents have been accurately recorded. This one in the sitting room of a storey-and-a-half farm house in Vermont has not. One would expect that, with so much light focused on so short and so recent a period of our history, Mr. Coolidge's inauguration would have been carefully chronicled with all the skill that modern newsmen and writers could bring to bear upon it.

Unfortunately for history, this is not the case.

For in the many accounts of the three minute episode which has, by its import and intensity, drawn thousands of Americans to this remote Vermont house, no two authors agree as to what precisely did happen.

This was, it seemed to me, an intriguing fact.

✳ 9

What odd quirk of fate could it have been, I asked myself, that caused so many errors and so many omissions in telling this story? Why did reputable and even well known writers apparently go off the deep end when they came to write about the simple and short inauguration of Calvin Coolidge at Plymouth Notch?

Why, indeed, did every individual who was there, or who heard the facts first hand, tell a different yarn?

---

[1]The natural beauty of the village nestled in the hills added, I think to, the charm. Robert A. Woods once wrote, "It is surrounded by green slopes which seem to run up into the sky . . . from the narrow level surface of the valley, the whole scene is impressive with its magnitude, its sense of ever-lasting foundations, of vast uplifting forces, of a command to thought and silence."

Well, of course, the individuals can be accounted for. People remember strange things. The frailty of human memory is notorious. It is human to want to achieve a place in history and to enlarge on that place.

But how about the articles in magazines and newspapers and even books, most of which are written by professional authors?

Certainly hard working professionals like William Allen White, author of many books in addition to two about Calvin Coolidge, don't intentionally make cardinal errors in dates and facts. Clearly such an astonishing series of conflicting facts and major errors that have existed these 37 years about this segment of Coolidge history cannot in all conscience be laid to the incompetence of writers. Writers who write for a living are not *that* careless.

The answer to this riddle, I now know, is to be found in quite another direction.

It was like this: All the writers in the course of doing research for their stories, naturally took the long, winding, hill road to Plymouth Notch right where the great event had taken place. They were looking for facts . . . first hand. But before they left the tiny village, they walked up the front steps of the Coolidge Homestead and knocked at the side door.

To each and every one of them, the door was opened ajar. Peeking out was a prim, spare, bird-like little woman.

This was Miss Aurora Pierce, the Coolidge housekeeper. She lived there. The Coolidge family came and went, but Miss Pierce never went.

The well known weakness of writers (who are, after all, incorrigibly romantic) for off-beat, odd and if possible unique characters, proved, I think, their downfall. Any writer worth his salt had only to glance quickly at the flinty, determined charm of this neat Vermont spinster to realize that here, indeed, was a natural. Here, patently, was the local color they had hoped to find.

(29)

As they looked upon the visage of Miss Aurora Pierce they all dropped, like hot rivets, any real facts that they had secured elsewhere and began straightway to listen to what they knew at once to be "a typical Vermont character."

From Miss Pierce they took everything she told them and they took it as Gospel truth. After all she'd been there, *she* did not deny, on that historic night of August 3, 1923, and she was there now!

She certainly was. Her sense of publicity was unprofessional. No more sheltered creature ever lived. In the 48 years she worked for the Coolidges she never ventured farther away than Rutland, 25 miles distant, and then only to buy some thread she couldn't find at home.

Yet to all persons approaching with a pad of paper and a pencil she was willing and often eager to tell them the whole story, in the most minute detail, of precisely what happened when Calvin was sworn in by his father, Colonel John Coolidge. Untrained as she was, her sense of public relations emerged as acute as it was sure. She knew she was considered by one and all as the only living fount of knowledge about Calvin Coolidge and his father. It was an accolade she could take pride in. And she did.

But the twist is this: To each and every one seeking knowledge she gave a slightly different story! How could this be, I asked myself? Especially when she had apparently seen it all happen and like every other Vermont spinster I have ever known, was never wrong! I determined to find out.

But first, I had to know more about Miss Pierce and her history.

Miss Pierce had hired out to Colonel John Coolidge, the President's father in 1908. By the time Carrie Brown Coolidge, the Colonel's second wife, who had never been too strong died in 1920, Aurora Pierce had got used to running things in the Coolidge house. From that day on she did run things and she ran them pretty much as she pleased.

After Colonel John died in 1926, Miss Pierce was the sole year-round occupant of this historic house. The President and his family came back summers as often as they could. After Mr. Coolidge died in 1933, Grace Coolidge continued to return with her son, John, and his family. But Miss Pierce was in charge.

The President had, in 1932, built a commodius two-and-a-half storey addition to the small original house. On the first floor of this addition he built a large living room, library and bedrooms; on the second, three more bedrooms. Here the family lived when they were in residence. This left Miss Pierce alone in the original house. Since there was no kitchen in the new part, everyone ate in the old kitchen. Here Aurora held sway, cooking on the ancient wood-burning iron range which she kept spic and span with stove-blacking. She took pride in it. She also never allowed a drop of water to stand in the cast iron sink after the dishes were done. It could easily rust.

From the decade after the Civil War when Miss Pierce had been born to the moment when this house became the best known village home in America, no changes had been made either in the house or in her operation of it or in her attitude toward it. Being a Vermonter and a spinster, Miss Pierce was determined that no changes ever would be made. A more outstanding example of Vermont frugality and independence of mind would be hard to find.

After Calvin became president, he had installed such suitable conveniences as a bathroom with flush toilet and running hot and cold water, an electric hot water heater, and oil stove and electric lights throughout the house.

But Miss Aurora Pierce continued to the end to stick to the known rather than to test the unknown. Up to the day of her death she heated water for washing in the woodstove reservoir, washed all the clothes by hand in a tin tub on a wood-ribbed scrub board, and kept the butter and milk down in the cool cellar in an earthenware crock. She also utilized the dry privy still attached to the house. All this she did to save the cost of electricity.

In spite of constant admonitions of Grace Coolidge that the minimum rate per month for electricity would assuredly more than cover all the current Miss Pierce could possibly use, Aurora also still insisted on carrying (much to Mrs. Coolidge's concern) a kerosene lamp from room to room and upstairs to her own bedroom on the second floor back.

The winter before Miss Pierce died, in spite of the arrangements made to have a man shovel snow, she was up on the precarious slanting roof of the front porch shoveling off the heavy fall of that year.

She was 87 years old.

�֍ 11

When the State took over the house after she died, we found that the back room next to the woodshed was filled to the ceiling with boxes and bushel baskets. In each basket were neatly piled strips of birch bark; in each box, chips. They might come in handy for starting fires. It was wasteful to throw them away.

I trust no one thinks I am poking fun. Today when we are used to buying everything with money in an age when apparently money can buy everything, I know it's difficult to

The other corner of the Kitchen showing the stove, iron sink, wood box and kerosene lamps.

comprehend an epoch when Vermonters enjoyed a habit of heart and mind, by which they obtained many things without money.

The foundation of Vermont frugality lay not in the miserly parsimony of saving money. It was largely to obtain and save things for which no money was ever paid!

Not that Aurora Pierce failed to save money.

I shall never forget the day John Coolidge and I went to talk to her about the State of Vermont taking over the historic house. She had worked for the family exactly 48 years. John knew she needed, and certainly ought to have a rest. There was no need, and had not been for years, of her doing all the work around the place.

I told her that the State would build, on the second storey, a nice apartment, with parlor, bedroom and bath, and a kitchen too, and that we would heat, light and maintain it at no cost to John. She could live there with comfort. No longer would she have to split wood, shovel snow, carry lamps, gather birch bark or go down the dark damp cellar stairs for the butter.

Of course she would have none of it!

She listened patiently while all this was explained. We were in hope that she would like what we wanted to do to make life easier for her. Then she said:

"Well, John, I guess I can go out and get a job!"

John said he didn't think that would be necessary.

Then I sat down on the old brown velvet covered couch in the kitchen where she was and took her hand.

"You are, Miss Pierce, the most favored woman in Vermont," I said.

I went on hurriedly, "You are! Why, what other woman has back of her the Coolidge family *and* the State of Vermont!"

She didn't answer me but she looked up to John, who was standing, and said:

"John, what be I going to do for clothes?"

If you work for 48 years in a house where everything is furnished; shelter, clothing and food . . . and you put every bit you get paid into the savings bank (then paying up to 6% compound interest) and you never take any out because there is no need to, you will, after nearly half a century accumulate a tidy sum. I believe that's what Miss Pierce had. Local gossip even had it, years before, that Aurora had tucked away more then $50,000. I can't prove it, but allowing for exaggeration, it was common gossip in the Notch that when she died she left almost $40,000., safely held in more than one sound Vermont savings bank.

It is an undoubted truth that Aurora Pierce had a mind of her own and she knew what she was doing. If anyone else had any notion about how things should properly be done in the Coolidge Homestead they had to cope with her.

Some light was shed on this fact by Earle S. Kinsley of Rutland, National Republican Committeeman from Vermont during Mr. Coolidge's presidency. We'll let Mr. Kinsley tell it:—

"The story begins early one morning in the summer of 1925," he relates in his published reminiscences, "It was the last day of trout season, I had caught a handsome mess in the ponds at my camp in Mendon, and knowing President Coolidge was spending a few days with his father at Plymouth, I hurriedly dressed my catch and drove over the mountain, arriving at the Coolidge farmhouse shortly before noon. As I approached it I found Colonel Coolidge sitting on the porch. I saluted him, 'Good morning, Colonel!' He responded, 'Mornin'.' I told him what I had brought, saying I thought the President would enjoy them for his noonday meal. The Colonel motioned with his head in the direction of the kitchen, and said, 'Miss Pierce is in there.'

"I passed through the dining room into the kitchen and greeted Miss Pierce with a 'Good morning, Miss Pierce, I have brought some nice trout for the President's dinner.' Her retort was, 'We're goin' to have beefsteak for dinner.' I persisted, 'Well, Miss Pierce, I caught them not more than two hours ago, and have them dressed and ready for the frying pan, and you know I have the reputation of cooking trout tastily, will you allow me to fry them?' She did not grant me permission, but I unwrapped the fish and placed them on the broad shelf. She glanced at them and exclaimed, 'Cut their heads and tails off.' I insisted that was not the proper form in which to cook trout, and inquired if she would give me a frying pan. She replied, 'The beefsteak's in it.'

"Apparently, sensing I was not to be scared away she approached the stove, removed the cover from the pan, stuck a fork into the leathery-over-cooked beefsteak, placed it on a platter and put it in the warming oven. After cleaning the pan I proceeded to cook the fish, during which time Miss Pierce made no comments and declined to enter into conversation. When the trout were ready to remove from the fire I requested a platter, and she said, 'The beefsteak's on the platter.' I then asked for a large plate, which she grudgingly furnished.

"As I was taking the fish out of the pan, Colonel Starling of the Secret Service Staff entered the kitchen by way of the shed door. Nonplussed at seeing me at the Colonel's kitchen stove, he blurted out, 'What you doing here?' Not waiting for my explanation he proceeded into the dining room and there gave me the 'high sign'. I joined him and told him my errand. He inquired if I wished to see the President, and before I could make answer, he advised me that the President had just returned from an appointment with his dentist at Woodstock, and that he had been administered novocaine, as a consequence of which treatment he was far from being in a good-natured mood. I left immediately.

"Some days later I received through the mail from Washington a box of Corona cigars, with the President's card enclosed, on which was inscribed, 'Many thanks for the trout. They were excellent.' "

For twenty-three years after President Coolidge's death, Miss Pierce was alone at the homestead except, as I have related, when the Coolidges came for their vacation and one other sporadic exception.

Some days in the summer, when she felt like it, she would unhasp the screen door from the porch into the sitting room and let the public in. Striding briskly from the door, she would walk over in front of the bay windows and sit down in a chair behind a card table. The tourists, slightly perplexed at this quick legerdemain, would step into the room and look around. It was sparsely furnished. There was the parlor stove with its black pipe running along the ceiling, three chairs, the secretary and an old couch covered with a faded cloth. Above the couch was a large framed photograph of Calvin Coolidge as Lieutenant Governor of Massachusetts.

The tourists would stand there a minute bewildered until suddenly they realized that the old lady was talking. She was telling exactly what had happened in this room on the night of August 3, 1923.

After relating the story hundreds of times one would expect Miss Pierce to have memorized a set speech, but strangely, it often varied in minor detail. One got the impression that the old lady's memory was failing. However, in the last few years of her life, she added a new touch. Grace Coolidge had been advised of the unique value to history of the kerosene lamp with the pot-bellied chimney, the family bible and the table cover that were used on that historic occasion. She took them to Northampton where she kept them in a fire-proof vault.

This action Miss Pierce did not think much of. From that day on, Aurora's speech had some things added. She would

Grace Coolidge, taken in the Adams House. This I consider one of the best likenesses of this remarkable woman.

(39)

come to the part of her story where Mr. Coolidge stepped up to the table to take the oath. There was a cloth on the table then. "Tain't there now. Mrs. Coolidge *took* it."

On the cloth that Mrs. Coolidge took was, of course, the famous lamp.

"Tain't there now. Mrs. Coolidge *took* it."

Beside the lamp was the Coolidge bible. Belonged to his mother. "Tain't there now.. Mrs. Coolidge *took* it."

After this talk, Miss Pierce would remain behind the card table. The astonished visitors would then start toward the door. But a nervous shuffling noise would attract them. They turned to see what was causing it. She was pushing around on the shiny table top an array of post cards and what looked like buttons, all of which, she soon informed them were for sale.

Hastening through the door and out onto the porch the tourists would exclaim to each other, that it was damned funny the Coolidge family had to resort to selling souvenirs in the President's home.[1] But a little reflection would soon reveal, of course, that the Coolidges didn't. Then one visitor would say to another:

"Wonder why the Coolidges *let* her do that?"

Little did they know that the truth lay just the other way around. It was never what the Coolidges, kind, considerate and never wanting to make a fuss about anything, *let* Miss Pierce do. It was what Miss Aurora Pierce let the Coolidges do!

One time, however . . . and *only* one time in her long life was the shoe on the other foot.

---

[1]As late as February, 1960, to demonstrate the vitality of the errors kept alive by Miss Pierce during her lifetime, an author from Massachusetts published a yarn on Coolidge's Plymouth and related that Miss Pierce had been promoted from housekeeper to caretaker", as well as revealing that Miss Pierce was selling souvenirs in order to "keep up the property". At the time of the President's death in 1933, it is said he left upwards of $250,000, an estate I am sure his widow invested prudently and carefully which upon her death in 1957 could easily have increased several fold. I doubt if the family needed any help in "keeping up the house".

One time, it was what the President of the United States decided to *let* Miss Pierce do.

And that is the point of my story.

This is my favorite picture of the President. He is not happy because he was made to pose, at the demands of photographers, to show that he had once been a fisherman. But here he senses the falseness of fishing in a formal suit, and straw hat, in a hay field, with no stream in half a mile. Lacking the banter of F. D. Roosevelt, he was never able, being a kind man, to outwit or circumvent many of the odd requests from the press, but he soon learned, as most politicians must, to suffer fools gladly.

Vermont's Congressman from the Second District, Republican Porter H. Dale, was campaigning early that year. In the round of visits covering the State he arrived in the evening of August 2, 1923, at the Adnabrown Hotel in Springfield. Awaiting him were Leonard L. Lane, president of the New England branch of the Railway Mail Clerk's Union, Joe Fountain, 21-year old editor of the *Springfield Reporter* (the local weekly) and Herbert Thompson, commander of Post No. 18, American Legion.[1]

After talking for awhile Joe Fountain suggested they walk across the street to the corner drug store for a drink. It was an unusually hot, uncomfortable evening. They had a drink of Moxie and a few minutes later started back to the hotel. Before they reached it, Fred Wheeler dashed out of his drug store yelling to them. He had news. He had just picked it up on his crystal radio set in the back room of his store.

President Harding had died in San Francisco.

The drama of this announcement was not lost on the newspaper man. Joe Fountain on entering the hotel was called to the telephone. It was G. B. Littlefield, head of the AP Bureau in Boston. Joe was correspondent for the Boston office. Littlefield said the President had died at 7:30 o'clock, western time. The flash was now going out on the AP wires. Joe better get to Plymouth.

---

[1]The last two, Fountain and Thompson, were living in New York City and Connecticut, respectively, in 1960. Several interviews as well as tape recordings with these gentlemen have furnished many of the intimate facts in my account.

Dale, a professional politician, sensed it in another way. He realized the import of this news to the vice president of the United States vacationing at Plymouth Notch, only 30 miles north. Dale said they ought to go to the Notch at once. Maybe there would be something they could do.

The four men ran across the street and luckily Captain Dan Barney was there, sitting in his taxicab. He agreed at once to drive them to Plymouth. They were excited as they started out. The big phaeton was being pushed to the limit. Thompson remembers vividly the refrain he heard above the roar of the engine and the noise of the road. Dale was trying to make himself heard.

"The United States has no president . . . no president!"

And it hadn't . . . for almost three hours.

The Congressman was too good a politician to miss the significance of timing. He knew there was no telephone in the Coolidge house and he guessed there wasn't one in the whole village. If they could reach the Notch and give Mr. Coolidge the news . . . why then . . .

Furthermore, perhaps something could be done about swearing in the president . . . maybe this very night.

Captain Barney pushed the throttle to the floor. The car reached 60 miles an hour. It did not take a long time to arrive in Ludlow, half way to Plymouth. Stopping at the hotel, Fountain found that William Playfair and John B. Knox of the Associated Press Bureau had left some time ago for Plymouth. News agencies and metroplitan papers had, upon the first news of President Harding's illness, assigned men to be near Plymouth just in case anything happened. Represented were the United Press, International News Service, Universal Service, as well as the New York *Times*, Washington *Post* and several others.

Slowing down on a blind curve for an approaching car, Barney stopped. The other car stopped. It was Knox and Playfair, returning from Plymouth. They said Mr. Coolidge had given them an important statement. It was no use to go

(43)

up there now: Mr. Coolidge had gone to bed. They were rushing back to Ludlow to file the story. They thought the vice president would take the oath of office the next day, so now, the show was over. The Coolidge statement read as follows:

"Reports have reached me, which I fear are correct, that President Harding is gone. This world has lost a great and good man. I mourn his loss. He was my chief and my friend. It will be my purpose to carry out policies which he has begun for the service of the American people and for meeting their responsibilities wherever they may arise. For this purpose I shall seek the cooperation of all those who have been associated with the President during his term of office. Those who have given their efforts to assist him I wish to remain in office, that they may assist me. I have faith that God will direct the destinies of our nation."

Joe Fountain and Congressman Dale took council.[1] They decided to go on to Plymouth anyway. It was only a hunch but it might pay off.

As they reached the sleeping village of Plymouth Notch there was a light showing in the Coolidge house! Dale was concerned. How could this be? They had just been told by Knox that the President had gone to bed. But maybe he hadn't!

Herbert Thompson remembers that he felt he was not dressed properly to be received by a President of the United States. As the party stepped up to the porch, Thompson decided to stay out there. Dale and Fountain went in, accompanied by Lane. Barney remained with Thompson. There was an old canvas hammock on the porch. They sat down on it.

At this moment, their eyes becoming accustomed to the dark, Thompson and Barney spied another car parked in the

---

[1]Joe H. Fountain, now Director of Public Relations for the Canadian National Railway, published an admirable little brochure some years ago entitled "Homestead Inaugural", in which he relates these and other experiences that night.

This picture shows John Coolidge, his mother, the President, his father Colonel John, leaving the church in front of the Homestead, after funeral services for Calvin Coolidge, Junior, who died in 1924 when Mr. Coolidge was President and is now buried in the Cemetery at Plymouth, next to his father.

road to the west of the house. Just then someone turned on its headlights.

They wondered who this could be. They never did find out that it was W. A. Perkins from Bridgewater, because he waited only a few seconds for another man to get in beside him and then, starting the car, drove off.

The nearest Western Union agent was Mrs. W. A. Perkins[1] at Bridgewater, eight miles north. Her full time job was manning the local telephone exchange in the front room of her house on the main street. At 11:30 that night the White River office had called her. They said they wanted her to take down a telegram from George B. Christian in San Francisco. It was addressed to Calvin Coolidge.

A second after she had written it down she stepped into the front hall and called to her husband asleep upstairs. She indicated no time was to be wasted. He wasted none. He was up and dressed quicker than he had ever been before. He left the house in such a hurry he didn't even take time to lace up his shoes. Backing his big 1918 Cole-8 out of the barn he started for Plymouth. He had the paper in his pocket.

Sleeping that night in a house a few feet away from Mrs. Perkins' telephone exchange was Clarence Blanchard, a resident of Plymouth. It was a hot night and the windows were wide open. Blanchard was awakened by the insistent ringing of the telephone. He went to his window and, because the houses were so close together, actually heard Mrs. Perkins in her excitement yell the news to her husband. Mr. Blanchard got up and rushed over to nearby Furman's Boarding House, figuring it was someone's duty to notify the President's secretary Erwin Geiser and chauffeur, Joseph McInerney, a govern-

[1]Mrs. Perkins, in 1959, gave me a lengthy interview followed by a written account of the part she played in the night-time drama.

ment employee who had been assigned to the vice president. They were stopping at Furman's Boarding House in Bridgewater because they could not find accommodations in Plymouth.

Getting dressed quickly, they rushed to the shed and started the Pierce Arrow, Model 80, which McInerney had driven up from Washington for the vice president. They started hell-bent up the narrow twisting dirt road for the Notch, in the excited belief that they were taking the famous message to the vice president.

But Mr. Perkins got there first by about three minutes. His wife was fond of telling in later years how he drove so fast that the speedometer never worked again!

There wasn't a single light in the village. Perkins drove up in front of the dark Coolidge house and knocked sharply. Colonel John soon came to the kitchen door in his night shirt. After asking Perkins to step in he thanked Perkins and walked into the sitting room. Here he opened the door to the stairway. He called, "Calvin!"

Calvin, who was sleeping with his wife in the bedroom at the head of the stairs, awoke at once (so his father remembered in later years) and stepped into the upstairs hall. He listened to what his father was saying. President Harding was dead!

Calvin Coolidge's reputation for frugality and laconic expression came from the fact that he never, like many other Vermonters, saw the use of saying anything when it was not necessary. If a man was excited, he might as well keep it to himself. On this night, and for several days and nights before, the nation was becoming increasingly alarmed over the news of President Harding's curious illness in the far west. The wire services and the press were excited. But if the vice president was, he didn't say. That night like many another night at Plymouth, he had calmly gone to bed at nine o'clock.

Calvin Coolidge, when his father had spoken, said, "Thank you, father", and went back to the bedroom. He spoke to his wife.

In the *Autobiography*, Calvin Coolidge, recalling this dramatic moment, had this to say about his father who had stood at the bottom of the stairs:

"I noticed that his voice trembled. As the only times I had observed that before were when death had visited our family, I knew that something of the gravest nature had occurred . . . he must have been moved also by the thought of the many sacrifices he had made to place me where I was, the twenty-five mile drives in storms and in zero weather over our mountain roads to carry me to the Academy and all the tenderness and care he had lavished upon me in the thirty-eight years since the death of my mother in the hope that I might sometime rise to a position of importance, which he now saw realized."

Mr. Perkins, now Colonel John had taken his message and left the room, quietly closed the kitchen door and walked back to his car. He then noticed a light come on in an upstairs room.

Calvin and his wife dressed at once. They they knelt down to pray.[1] Colonel John had gone back into the kitchen. Bessie Pratt was building a fire in the stove.

Mr. Perkins had now reached his car when he saw the headlights of another vehicle approaching around the corner of the Wilder house. Mr. Perkins waited. He did not know that it was McInerney and Geiser in the Pierce Arrow coming from Bridgewater. And of course, neither did Joseph McInerney, the president's chauffeur, and secretary Edwin Geiser know who was in the big Cole 8, with the lights on.

---

[1]Mr. Coolidge was not, in his lifetime, an ardent church goer, but some facets of his life revealed his belief in destiny. Once, he was asked when he first decided on a public career. He replied that he had never decided: his intention was to be a lawyer. "Of course," he said, "when I became Lieutenant Governor, I wanted to be Governor." The reporter then said, "But the steps in your progress as an incumbent of public office have followed so inevitably as to suggest that there must have been a purpose in it." The president answered without a change of tone or emphasis, "There was a purpose in it; but it was not mine." *Robert A. Wood's* "The Preparation of Calvin Coolidge."

Mr. Coolidge didn't like to pose for photographers doing things he was not accustomed to; but haying was a job he knew and liked and in this picture he was doing what came natural.

16

The news of President Harding's strange illness had certainly alerted the country's press. Wire service men, reporters and feature writers had been swarming around Plymouth Notch but none was actually staying there because there were no accommodations. Most of them were stopping in Ludlow, Bridgewater and nearby villages. When the flash reached them of Harding's death, they knew no time was to be lost. They all started for Plymouth.

Like the thousands of ancestors who by their descendants claim, came over in the Mayflower, dozens of people later claimed they were in Plymouth that night. As Joe Fountain has amusingly remarked, "It beats all how many people want to get into history by the back door." However, as Joe himself has related, William E. Playfair of the Boston AP Bureau was there with John B. Knox of the same office. Paul R. Mallon of the United Press was surely present. There is a yarn that one of them, when he got the news, rushed back to Ludlow so fast that he ran down a cow in Tyson. Others placed at the spot were James Hagerty of the New York *Times*, father of President Eisenhower's press secretary, and Francis Stevenson of the New York *News*.

They had all converged on the village from both directions; roads only came in from the north and the south. The still night was now disturbed by the chugging and an occasional backfire of automobiles. It was now about midnight.

"Good morning, Mr. President," one of them said. Mr. Coolidge did not reply to this. He had risen only a few minutes before. It wasn't exactly morning!

Mr. Perkins, outside in his car, was confused. He had turned on the car lights and was about to start when the Pierce Arrow stopped and disgorged two fast moving figures who lost no time in disappearing into the house. He thought he might now get back to Bridgewater and get some sleep. Although this was his wife's doings, he had, he reflected, beaten them all and got there first . . . by a neck. Those two men who just went in would find that out soon enough. Colonel Coolidge would tell them, soon as they closed the kitchen door.

Joseph McInerney[1] and Edwin Geiser soon discovered that they had missed delivering the message of Harding's death to the boss by only a few minutes.

But Geiser's arrival was fortuitous. He was just in time to take down in shorthand (at the boss's dictation) and to type out a message on the machine he had been using the day before in the dining room. As he was doing this, Mrs. Coolidge held the kerosene lamp over his shoulder. He had hardly finished before the newspaper men burst into the room and greeted Mr. Coolidge. They were told to wait:—an official statement would be ready in just a minute. It would be the first statement of the new president of the United States.

Only Mr. Coolidge wasn't technically or legally the new president. He hadn't taken the oath of office.

Mr. Perkins didn't know this: he was impatient to get home. As he took hold of the wheel with the engine running and got ready to double clutch, one of the reporters, Paul R. Mallon, begged a ride back to Bridgewater. Mr. Perkins said, "All right."

Paul Mallon convinced Mr. Perkins that he was in a hurry . . . a big hurry. The President's message must be telephoned in. Perkins said his wife was telephone operator at Bridge-

---

[1]McInerney was in 1960 living in Connecticut. During the summer of 1958 he had been hired as caretaker to the state-owned Coolidge homestead. From dozens of interviews and tape recordings, I have gleaned much background information from the former Coolidge chauffeur. Geiser died many years ago.

water. The two lost no time in getting back to Bridgewater. They arrived just before one o'clock and Mallon started at once to tie up the only telephone circuit out of the place. His first toll ticket, Mrs. Perkins recalls, was dated 1 A. M. As his later career demonstrated, Mr. Mallon was a successful and enterprising newspaper man. He proved it that night by managing to keep this one circuit tied up until 4 o'clock.

Mrs. Perkins remembers that several other reporters arrived in Bridgewater a few minutes later and found to their chagrin that Paul Mallon had not only preempted the one line but had beaten them all by getting his news out first.

But there was one newspaper man even smarter than Mallon. This was Joe Fountain. He was young and inexperienced, but he had a good hunch that back there at the Coolidge house in Plymouth Notch, something else might happen. While all the older, famous reporters from the cities had driven off in great excitement to file their stories recounting the first words of the 30th President of the United States, Joe Fountain decided to stick around.

Mr. Coolidge wasn't president yet!

✳ 17

The other reporters had all gone now, every one of them. They had figured the show was over! Things were dead quiet. As young Herb Thompson and taxi driver Barney sat swinging their feet from the porch hammock they talked in hushed voices. They wondered what the Congressman and Joe Fountain were doing in the house so long. It seemed like hours.

But it wasn't . . . it was only minutes. Pretty soon Joe McInerney stepped through the kitchen door onto the porch and walked rapidly past the two in the hammock. He had been ordered to go to the store.

McInerney was going on an important errand. Mr. Coolidge had called him into the room from the kitchen and said: "Joseph, go over and get that woman up." Joe somehow knew the boss could only be referring to Miss Florence Cilley who owned the store. She was a newcomer; she's lived in town less than twenty years.

Joe pounded on the store door and windows. Nothing happened. Then he went around back and pounded on the windows of the house where Miss Cilley was sleeping. Pretty soon she got up, went into the store and let him in the front door. She had lighted the kerosene lamp in her hand. She sat it down on the counter. She was alone:—like Miss Pierce, she was a spinster. As McInerney walked in a telephone was ringing incessantly. The operator was impatient: she had been trying to arouse someone for quite a few minutes.

It was former Governor Percival W. Clement of Rutland. When Clement had been, years before, president of the Rutland Railroad he had provided his private palace car to take Theodore Roosevelt to Buffalo. He was still a director of the railroad. He was also owner of the Rutland *Herald* and was by this hour aware of Harding's death. Because he had known Coolidge when Coolidge was Governor of Massachusetts, and had in fact as Governor of Vermont sent guns to Coolidge at the time of the Boston Police Strike, Clement would naturally want to be the first to help the new president.

He felt confident that he could offer his friend the private car of the Rutland Railroad, and if wanted, a private train the next day.

This was the message he gave McInerney.

This intelligence McInerney rushed back to Mr. Coolidge at the house. Mr. Coolidge said that there was no need for any special train. "I could just as well ride in the coach," he added, But there was no need to hurt Governor Clement's feelings:—if the railroad men wanted him to use the private car, why all right . . . hitch it on to the regular down-local in the morning and he would ride in it.

When Joe McInerney returned to the house from the store after relaying this message, Mr. Coolidge said he would like to make a call himself, now that Miss Cilley was up.

Edwin Geiser accompanied his boss to the store. Mr. Coolidge reached Attorney General Harry M. Dougherty. It was necessary to find out the exact words of the oath of office of the President of the United States. The secretary took down this conversation in shorthand. Mr. Coolidge then gave Miss Cilley some dollar bills to pay whatever the toll charges might be. One of these Miss Cilley had framed and displayed in her store as the first money spent by the new President.

Only he wasn't at that moment President. Mr. Coolidge went back to his house. It was nearing two o'clock.

It certainly was close:—tomorrow was going to be a scorcher all right.

The Oath-of-Office Room in the Coolidge Homestead. Mr. Coolidge stood at this table when he took the oath of office by the light of the kerosene lamp at 2.47 in the morning of Aug. 3, 1923.

✳ 18

In the Coolidge sitting room by the light of the single oil lamp Mr. Dale was now talking. Joe Fountain listened with admiration. The Congressman, he thought, was surely eloquent. Also persuasive.

"The United States, Mr. Coolidge, has no president. Why can't you take the oath of office right here? It isn't right that the United States should have no president!"

Mr. Coolidge guessed that it wasn't. He was recalling what the Attorney General had just told him. There appeared to be nothing in this conversation to deny Dale's assertion. Yet he hesitated. Mr. Coolidge was a lawyer. Who would give him the oath? This traditional rite belonged to the Chief Justice of the United States. He was in Washington.

"Your father . . . he's a government official. He's a notary public."

This unique family picture is one of the few showing Calvin Coolidge, Junior (who died in 1924) taken in the summer when the family was at Plymouth.

Colonel John said that was perfectly true, he was a notary. He had a commission signed by Governor Hartness of Vermont, to prove it. He probably could give the oath, all right.[1]

But what was this oath?

They now had it from two sources. The attorney general's telephone message and in a book of Vermont Statutes which Colonel John, his son's wife and Dale had discovered when Mr. Coolidge was telephoning at the store. Here it was printed in black and white: it proved that the telephone message was correct. Geiser was ordered to type, immediately, the words of the oath and to make three copies. Mr. Coolidge then told his secretary just how he wanted these copies made. Each, he instructed, was to be typed on a piece of paper two inches wide. No use wasting paper!

Mr. Coolidge took the three strips of paper and laid them down on the oval table near the bay window. On this was the only illumination in the room. It was a kerosene lamp with an etched pot-bellied glass chimney and a glass fount known for years by antique collectors as the "Lincoln Drape". Its design was in the form of the Lincoln funeral drapes.[2]

Standing back of the table was Colonel John. He was ready. He had on his black Sunday coat, a white shirt and a black necktie. At Mr. Coolidge's left was his wife, Grace, at his right Congressman Porter Dale. Nearby stood Joe Fountain and Edwin Geiser. Standing a little back was L. L. Lane. Near the kitchen door was Joe McInerney.

---

[1]Years later in talking about this occasion Colonel John was asked, "Colonel, how did you know you could give the presidential oath of office to your son?" To which the old man replied, "Well, I didn't know that I couldn't."

[2]Today this style lamp is known to glass collectors as the "Coolidge Drape". In later years when not too careful reporters recounted the event in newspapers, they invariably said the room was lighted by "a flickering flame from a dirty oil lamp . . ." This always made Miss Pierce angry. She said *her* lamps never flickered because they were trimmed the way they ought to be. Certainly, she snorted, *her* lamps were never dirty! And, of course, in this she was absolutely correct.

In the kitchen was a woman.

On the porch which opened directly into this sitting room stood Herbert Thompson and Dan Barney. They had slid off the hammock, walked over and were now pressing their noses against the screen door. This ludicrous picture caused a slight diversion.

Mr. Coolidge turned to Dale.

"Who are these men on the piazza?"

Mr. Dale told him. This seemed to satisfy him.

Mrs. Coolidge then said: "Calvin, are you going to wait until the newspaper reporters get back?" She recalled how quickly they had all rushed off, all except Joe Fountain.

He said he wasn't. They went of their own accord, didn't they! His father, he now observed, had one of the two-inch wide pieces of paper in his hand. He was bending over in order to hold the paper near the lamp. The vice president now turned to his father. In an unfaltering voice the old man began to read the typed words:

"I do solemnly swear that I will faithfully execute . . ." he stopped. His son repeated, "I do solemnly swear that I will faithfully execute . . ."

"the office of President of the United States . ."

"the office of President of the United States . ."

"and I will to the best of my ability preserve . ."

"and I will to the best of my ability preserve . ."

"protect and defend the Constitution of the United States."

"protect and defend the Constitution of the United States."

The son stopped a second and then in a firm, determined voice, added four words:

"So help me God."

The President of the United States now drew up the only arm chair in the room and sat down at the table.

Moving his mother's bible slightly to one side, he took the steel pen his father passed to him and signed all three copies of the oath that Erwin Geiser had typed. His father remarked that this pen had been in the family for over 50 years. The President made no comment. He laid the pen down and rose.

Mr. Dale had his hunter's case watch out of his vest pocket. He remarked that it was exactly 2:47.

It was going to be another muggy day . . .

The President and Mrs. Coolidge examining the carriage in which he was wheeled as a baby at Plymouth.

At 2:50 the President stepped back into the shadows of the room and opening the door upstairs, waited for Grace Coolidge to go ahead. He turned to the others in the room and said, "Good night."

Just then automobile headlights glared into the bay window of the darkened room. More cars had driven up.[1]

The President and his wife paused.

Circuit engineer Booth of the telephone company had received at midnight the flash about Harding's death. He knew exactly what he had to do but it would take a little while to do it. He got hold of District Plant Chief, W. T. Durfee, in Rutland. Durfee aroused Edmond E. Blakely, a lineman. They found an instrument, wires and tools and started for Plymouth Notch as fast as they could drive.

At just about the same second Wire Chief, Robert A. Doray and Toll Testman, Charles W. Sawyer also left White River Junction, with coils of wire and tools to connect up telegraphic press service. Both hit the target together . . . in two cars.[2]

The men entered the kitchen. The President, looking through the door, was intrigued. He stepped into the kitchen. With his permission they prepared to install an instrument.

---

[1]A few seconds before, Joe Fountain had rushed back to Springfield to file his story. Barney, Thompson and Dale went with him.

[2]The story of these installations is told in a contemporary article in "Telephone Topics", a publication of the *New England Telephone Company*, and confirmed by notes made by Judge George Jones, at the time.

The President is directing his son John in the job of getting shingles into the woodshed. Through the open shed door was the horse stall. This is now the visitors' entrance to the Coolidge Homestead.

Colonel John stood by saying nothing. But he was thinking. He had resisted for years and years the blandishments of telephone salesmen who had insisted that he of all men ought to have a telephone:—his son had been Lieutenant Governor, Governor and Vice President. But Colonel John had stoutly declared he wouldn't tolerate one of the things in the house! What was more he wouldn't take one even if it were put in free.

But now . . . well, maybe Calvin, being President of the United States, would need one. So let it go![1]

How busy the telephone men were!

The Colonel was slightly amused at the glee with which the telephone men got to work. Also he had to admit it was rather odd to see how interested his son appeared to be. Even his daughter-in-law, Grace, wanted to help. All this excitement over a telephone! The workmen had found that the main toll line between Rutland and White River passed near enough the house to cut into toll section No. 142 with a temporary drop line running to a tree and thence through the kitchen window in the house. Colonel John saw Grace holding one of the kitchen lamps to light Doray's job of mounting the wall instrument to the front window casing. By 3:30 the telephone was ready.

The President never had posed and he wasn't going to start now. These men had worked so hard that it seemed a pity not to use the instrument. He would use it.

At exactly 3:35 he turned the crank on the side of the box, lifted the receiver off its hook and was soon through on a direct connection to the Secretary of State.

Of course it was no longer any emergency. But the President did believe that maybe Mr. Hughes might like to know . . .

He hung the receiver back on the hook. He had used the telephone. Everyone now seemed satisfied.

The President thought now, probably, he could go to bed.

Just at this moment more headlights brightened the room. Who was coming now?

---

[1]The first chore Colonel John did later in the morning after his son left for Rutland, was to use the telephone to call the central and tell them he wanted it taken out at once.

This haying picture shows the President sharpening the scythe with the whetstone, in back of the Coolidge Homestead. This, as well as pitching hay, was a job he well knew from many summers on the farm as a boy.

The President and his wife riding in the official car, a Pierce Arrow phaeton.

※ 20

It turned out to be the Jones brothers.

George F. Jones had worked as a cub reporter for the Rutland *Herald* while in college and had become by 1919, city editor. In 1922, deciding to follow the family tradition, he had been admitted to the Vermont bar but still retained his interest in newspaper work. He occasionally wrote stories as a free lance for the *Herald* and other papers, but was more often found assisting his friend, Arthur Granger, of the *Herald's* permanent staff. In 1923 Granger was also acting as stringer for the Boston *Globe*.

Just before two o'clock in the morning of August 3, 1923, George was haled out of bed by a telephone call from Granger. Granger reported in breathless haste that Mike Hennessey,[1] political reporter for the Boston *Globe* had been in touch with him. Hennessey, along with other pressmen had been waiting near Plymouth for several days for something to happen. He had just learned of the sudden illness of his wife in Boston so must return home immediately. In the meantime would Granger take over and go to Plymouth at once? Hennessey had heard the mid-night flash of Harding's death and knew that there might be a story at Plymouth Notch. The *Globe* must get this story.

Because he did not want to go alone, Granger asked George Jones if he'd take the family car and go along. George was delighted. He hadn't got the newspaper ink out of his blood.[2]

---

[1] A year later Hennessey published a book on Coolidge entitled "Calvin Coolidge: from a Green Mountain Farm to the White House."

[2] Jones became Probate Judge of Rutland County in 1943 and still occupies this office.

George lost no time in getting dressed, awakening his brother Lawrence[1] and starting the car. On the way to pick up Granger they found the gas tank nearly empty. There were few gas stations in 1923. It took some time to get the tank filled. By the time they got out of Rutland and on their way to Plymouth it was after two o'clock. Even at that, they had lost no time. But Plymouth was still a good 40 minutes drive.

The Jones boys with their friend, Granger, arrived in front of the Coolidge home in the Notch at just 3 o'clock. There was a light in the front room. Some men were on the porch.

One of the men they knew. It was Leonard L. Lane. He was seated in the hammock holding a tiny revolver in one hand. Lawrence asked about the gun.

George said the gun was so small Lane could hold it in the hollow of his hand and that's where he was holding it.

"I'm guarding Mr. Coolidge." Lane informed them. "I'm the only federal official on hand." The Jones boys recalled that Lane was a railway mail clerk and had something to do with the Postal Clerk's Union.

Lane offered the information that Mr. and Mrs. Coolidge were inside with Congressman Dale. Everyone else had gone, he added. George did not ask who everyone else was. He opened the screen door and went in. Lawrence and Granger remained on the porch talking to Lane and the chauffeur, Joe McInerney. Granger thought there was going to be a good story from these fellows because they had witnessed what had happened.

As they talked, two other men started to approach the house with telephone wires.

---

[1]Lawrence Jones later served five terms as Attorney General of Vermont.

In the front room George was greeted by Mr. Coolidge. He had met the vice president several times before. As a newsman he had been present at the Republican National Convention in 1920 when Governor Coolidge received the nomination as vice president. After the nomination, Coolidge had returned to Plymouth to visit his father and on July 4th, the President's birthday, George Jones had been sent to the Notch to interview the candidate. Later in the summer there had been two other meetings.

"Mr. Jones," said the President, "I believe you are the first newspaper reporter here since I took the oath."

He then returned to the back of the room to continue his conversation with Mr. Dale and his secretary, Edwin Geiser. Mrs. Coolidge asked George to sit down.

George sat down in the arm chair by the table near the bay window.

He then heard snatches of the conversation while talking to Mrs. Coolidge. The President was saying:

"I'd just as soon take the Pullman."

"They want you to take the private car." said Dale.

The President then repeated what he had told McInerney earlier. If they wanted to hitch the private car onto the down-local he would ride in it.

At this point George heard Secretary Geiser make some remark indicating he was surprised that Vermont railroads had Pullman private cars. Whether the poor man made this remark in jest or to get information it was difficult to tell because Mr. Coolidge immediately jumped on him and in no uncertain terms, informed him that Vermont was not the backwoods. Certainly they had Pullman private cars! He also

John Coolidge, with his father and mother on the observation platform of a private car, returning to Washington after the funeral of his grandfather, Colonel John Coolidge, who died in 1926.

informed his secretary that the former President of the Pullman Company lived in Manchester, Vermont. *His* name was Robert Todd Lincoln! *His* father was Abraham Lincoln!

Mr. Geiser offered no further comment. George then recalls that Mr. Coolidge said, "Nevertheless . . . I sent word to Governor Clement[1] that I would ride in the private car and I will. We'll leave here in the morning."

George turned his attention to the President's wife. She was telling him about the small slips of paper on the table. On one were typed the words of the oath of office of the President, and below some signatures. George made a note of them.

The names were Calvin Coolidge, Grace G. Coolidge, John Coolidge, Porter H. Dale, L. L. Lane, Joe H. Fountain, Edwin C. Geiser, Joseph M. McInerney.[2]

The President then came over and told George about where these people were standing during the ceremony. George made a rough diagram, as Mr. Coolidge talked. The President did not mention Joe Fountain, either at this point or six years later in the autobiography. The plain truth of the matter was, he did not know the young newspaper man who had stood in the room during the brief ceremony. Joe Fountain was barely of age; the President had never seen him before and he simply forgot such a person was there.[3] In saying that his chauffeur, McInerney, stood in front of the window, Mr. Coolidge was getting him mixed up with Fountain. It was Fountain who stood next to Dale and it was the chauffeur who stood in the shadows in back of the room.

This accounted for the fact that the President did not mention Fountain in his conversation with George Jones, or tell Jones that Fountain had left with a newspaper story. George, from the President's greeting, thought that he was the first newspaper reporter to arrive after the ceremony and supposed, in his excitement, that he was the first newspaper man to have *any* story.

As he was reading the names, George noticed that Colonel John Coolidge was not in the room.

"He said he wanted to take a walk," Mrs. Coolidge explained. "He's out doors somewhere."

George asked, "What time do you think the President will leave for Washington?"

---

[1]Percival W. Clement was Governor of Vermont from 1919 to 1921.

[2]This original and unique document has disappeared. It is not, according to the officials of the Library of Congress, in the Coolidge Presidential Collection in that Library. It is not in the papers left by Mrs. Coolidge at her death in 1957. No results have been obtained in trying to discover whether it was in the papers left by Edwin Geiser upon his death.

[3]Further, Joe Fountain left so quickly after the ceremony that the President did not see him at that time.

Mrs. Coolidge seemed puzzled. "Why, the President is dead!" she said.

Ten minutes was too short a time for her to accept the fact that her husband was President of the United States. She then smiled and told George that they were planning to leave on the morning train from Rutland.

With the few notes and the diagram sketch in his hand, George excused himself and went out onto the porch again. It was 3:20. Granger said no time was to be lost:—they had to get to Ludlow and file the story. George thought it was *his* story Granger was talking about but Granger was talking about the story he had got from Lane and McInerney.

The ten miles to Ludlow were covered in about 20 minutes.

On the way Granger asked, "What were you doing in there so long? You sure missed something. I got the whole story. Those two men on the porch saw it happen. We missed being there by ten minutes."

George laughed. "Gee . . . Art, I was working, I got the story too."

"Who'd you get it from?"

"I got it from the President and Mrs. Coolidge!"

"I'll be damned." was all that Granger could say.

But he soon added, "We'll get to a phone fast ."

It was about quarter of four when they reached Ludlow and a telephone. Granger started talking to the *Globe*. He said he now had the story Mike Hennessey wanted him to get.

"Just a minute," the voice replied . . . "I want to get the other boys on." Apparently a rewrite man and the night editor came on. Granger then handed the ear phone to George.

"You tell 'em . . ." Granger said. "You got it from the horse's mouth."

George was astonished but he stepped up to the phone and started to talk. A voice said, "Wait a sec . . . is this Granger?"

"Sure is," said George, knowing now he was expected to file under Granger's name as it was Granger's job. But it turned out to be a three man job. George told it, Granger got

(70)

the credit, and Mike Hennessey got the by-line in the morning *Globe*. But later, Granger divided the pay the *Globe* had sent him for the scoop. George got half . . . $15.00.

George was elated. He didn't much care then who got the credit. He and Granger had, he thought, scooped the world press with the first story of the unique Vermont inauguration in the village home.

About an hour earlier, Joe Fountain had reached his home base of Springfield and filed the story with the Associated

Mr. Coolidge with his wife, at right. In the center his wife's Aunt Gracia Moor (Wilder) who lived in the Wilder House. The morning walk was interrupted by the photographer in front of the Wilder House, with the church in the background.

Press. Just about the minute George hung up the telephone, the wire service had started to send out the actual first story of the great event to its members. This was Joe Fountain's story . . . no doubt about it. But George Jones did not know it until the next day.

✻ 22

They started back to the Notch. As they reached the Coolidge home, false dawn was beginning to show in the east. It was about 4:30. Some people were standing around in the Coolidge home. The local people had apparently heard the news. In the front room, the dim rays of the kerosene lamp could be seen through the bay window.

Now there was a light in the kitchen.

The three men entered this room. The President, Colonel John said, had retired. They found, talking with Colonel John, three men they knew: Judge Ernest E. Moore,[1] Winfield Sargent and Henry T. Brown, friends of Judge Moore.

Colonel John informed everyone that he wasn't tired, hadn't been in bed and wasn't going to bed. Moore and his friends had arrived very soon after the Jones brothers and Granger had left for Ludlow. They decided to stay until the President got up. Colonel John calculated Cal would get up about seven: had to, if he wanted to get to Rutland to catch the local.

The men in the kitchen now held a council of war, as Judge Moore later told it, and made plans. Some thought of one

---

[1]Mr. Moore had become Probate Judge of Windsor County in 1921 and in 1960 still holds that office.

thing, others of another until soon Moore was using the telephone to call U. S. Marshal, Albert M. Harvey of Chester, who he thought ought to know.

Judge Moore then said to no one in particular; "I've been trying for quite a spell to get someone on this phone . . . somebody on the Rutland. Can't seem to." He was talking about the Rutland Railroad.

"Figured we ought to see about a Pullman car for Cal."

George offered the information that the man to talk to was the general superintendent of the road . . . George L. R. French.

"You know him?"

"Sure I know him."

"All right . . . go ahead and see if you can get him on that phone."

George stepped up to the newly installed telephone. Colonel John watched but uttered no word about the instrument. It was there, in plain sight, on the front wall of the kitchen. The operator who answered was alert. She had handled a very important call from the President only an hour or so ago. She could handle this one.

Mr. French was routed out of bed. He hadn't heard the news. He thought something could be arranged.

No one told him, of course, that Mr. Clement had made all the arrangements.

Moore got back on the telephone and routed Governor Redfield Proctor out of bed, telling him the news and urging him to meet the President's party at the private car in the morning. He later reached the Mayor of Rutland with additional suggestions for proper police protection for the new President.

※ 23

It was now so light outdoors that the Colonel blew out the lamps. As he was doing this, another car drove in front of the house and out rushed a man who proved to be U. S. Marshal Harvey.

Harvey was late. When he first got the message he was busy chasing bootleggers and thought that the call from Plymouth was a false alarm trumped up to disuade him from catching the criminals. Now he knew better.

He took charge at once. Lane was no longer the only federal official present. Harvey added to the roster by dubbing the men in the kitchen deputies.[1] They could act as a body guard for the President on his way to Rutland.

Just about this time Aurora Pierce came into the kitchen. This was her regular time to get up. She didn't return the greetings of the men in her kitchen, but started to get breakfast. She was now having the honor of getting the first meal to be eaten by the new President but she didn't know it.[2]

---

[1]This included Ernest Moore, George Jones, his brother, Lawrence, Winfield Sargent, Henry Brown and Clarence E. Blanchard who had joined the group just before Harvey arrived.

[2]McInerney told me in 1957 that as he came into the kitchen, after getting a few hours sleep upstairs in the boys' room (which Colonel John had assigned him) Miss Pierce was there finishing her preparations for breakfast. He greeted her but said no more. As the rest entered the room and sat down at the table, no word was spoken by anyone about the events of four hours earlier and certainly Miss Pierce asked no questions. I asked him why. He said she told him later she felt it was none of her business: if they had wanted her to know they would have told her.

Years later, upon being interviewed by Joe Fountain, she told him this repast consisted of rice, wheat cereal, bacon, fried potatoes, rolls and doughnuts. As she was telling the story, Colonel John reminded her she had forgotten something. "Didn't we have pickles that morning?" he asked. "Course we did," she snapped, ". . . always have pickles on the table."

But for the first time in her years of serving this family, there was one morning chore she did not this morning have to accomplish; the fire was already going merrily in the range.

At exactly seven, President and Mrs. Coolidge came into the kitchen. They promptly sat down at the table. Aurora served the breakfast.

Outside, on the porch, Marshall Harvey was organizing his task force. The sun was up and more people were hovering around. Some of them kept interrupting the Marshal. He was having a hard time getting his orders heard.

He told his deputies he would ride on the front seat of the President's Pierce Arrow with the chauffeur, McInerney and naturally this car would lead the procession. The next car would take deputies Lawrence Jones, Sargent, and Brown. Bringing up the rear would be Moore in his car, accompanied by Clarence Blanchard. George Jones would, the minute the President got packed, take all the luggage in his car and start for Rutland, meeting the party at the railway depot.

The Marshal was warning all hands not to let anyone pass. "Don't you dare let anyone get by . . . don't care who it is . . . stop 'em. Stop 'em anyway you have to."

They said they would. Whereupon Marshal distributed pistols he had brought along. The new deputies felt very serious about their official duties now.

* 24

By the time the President and his wife came out and entered the Pierce Arrow, it was a little after 7:30. The procession lined up as Harvey had ordered and started out of the village. When they got to Allen Brown's house, they all waited while McInerney drove the President's car down the short narrow road to the Plymouth Notch Cemetery. Here the President walked up the hill and stood silently before his mother's grave. His wife stood at his side.

The procession soon reformed. At Mt. Holly three loose hogs belonging to Pat Stewart ran into the road, helter skelter, in front of the President's car. McInerney acted quickly and managed to keep from running the car off the road.[1]

Soon after this incident, a car came up fast behind the procession and tried to pass. The deputies obeyed orders and forced the stranger off the road. Horns started to blow. All cars stopped.

The excited U. S. Marshal came running back to see who had dared to pass. He soon found out another and higher ranking federal official was now on hand. It was A. L. Mc-Cormack of the Department of Justice. He had been ordered to get there fast and guard the new President. He wasn't very happy. He didn't like being pushed off the road. The President spoke to him and the procession got off to another start.

The President entered the Rutland Railroad Private Car at 9:25 and the train pulled out in a few minutes. The car had been hitched to the down local at Mr. Coolidge's request. This was the milk train that had to stop at every station and flag stop.

The President and Mrs. Coolidge found waiting for them former Governor Clement, George French, the then Vermont Governor Redfield Proctor, Earle Kinsley, Republican National Committeeman from Vermont, Howard L. Hindley, editor of the Rutland *Herald*, and Dr. Schuyler Hammond, the Rutland Railroad physician.

George Jones got aboard and sat in the smoker: here he found about twenty other newspaper men.

As the President went into his private car he said he did not want to see anyone. He felt he wanted some privacy.

---

[1]Pat Stewart, an ardent Democrat, put up a fuss about his dead hog, but Judge Moore told him to forget it; he was probably the only Democrat in history to have a hog killed by a Republican President.

He did not, then, as of course he would later have to, reckon with the classic attitude of the press against privacy.

The crew of the famous train were Thoms J. Mangan, engineer, Robert Stearns, fireman, William E. Amblo, conductor, H. A. Whitcomb, flagman, and C. V. Houston, traveling fireman. W. E. Elder, traveling engineer, William McBridge, trainman, and James Pilon, baggageman, made up the crew.

As the train passed Wallingford, a crowd was waiting at the depot to watch the President's car go by.

The newsmen in the smoker were urging the Secret Serviceman, McCormack, to let them into the President's car for a press conference.

The first press conference of the new President took place at about 11:30 that morning. George Jones, at McCormack's orders, stood at the door of the Coolidge car and identified the newsmen as they went in.

The President did not say much. He recalled that President Harding had fortunately invited him, as Vice President, to sit in the cabinet meetings. The brash questions of the press continued:—What was the new President going to do? What plans did he have for his administration? Mr. Coolidge could not answer. After all, he had been President less than eight hours, four of which he had been asleep.

President and Mrs. Coolidge at Plymouth Notch, July 4, 1931. On this day, his birthday, Mr. Coolidge had dedicated the flagpole near the granite marker in the village.

IV

LET HER SLEEP

The end of the story is about Miss Pierce.

Way back in this long, busy and very hot night Colonel John had, as related, lifted his voice to wake up his son sleeping in the best bedroom upstairs. Beyond the Coolidge's room was the bedroom of Aurora Pierce. The Colonel's voice must have awakened Miss Pierce.

Certainly it awakened Bessie Pratt. Bessie, a local resident, was often called in to help out when a lot of folks were there. She had been helping for several days during Calvin's visit this summer and was also sleeping in the house. She got up.

She went into the dark kitchen and lit two lamps; one she put on the shelf above the sink, the other on the kitchen table she had carefully, the night before, set for breakfast.[1]

Now, by the light of the two lamps, Bessie Pratt lost no time in building a good fire in the kitchen range and putting on

---

[1]No Vermonters over fifty years old would be curious about this. It was always a rural custom (and still is in some places) for good housekeepers to wash the dishes after a meal and set them right back on the table. The plates and cups were turned bottom-side up to keep them from getting dusty. Spoons were always thrust into a glass vase and other silverware laid beside the plates. This made everything spic and span for the next meal.

It also saved time.

the teakettle full of water. It was a hot night all right. She didn't know exactly what had happened to get Colonel John up at this unearthly hour but since he was up she knew he would need water to shave with.

Colonel John now came into the kitchen from his bedroom back of the sitting room. He now told her what had happened. He then filled his shaving mug with hot water. He took it to the mirror on the wall and by the light of the kerosene lamp he shaved. Then he went back to his bedroom, put on a black coat and tie and entered the sitting room. He helped Grace and Dale find the book with the presidential oath in it. He discussed the idea of giving his son the oath.

* 26

At about 2:30, Calvin and Grace, Congressman Dale, Joe Fountain, Edwin Geiser, McInerney, and Lane stood waiting. They heard Grace speak to Calvin.

"Yes," Grace said, "Everyone is here now."

But wait a minute! Everyone wasn't. No one had apparently given the missing person a thought until now, over two hours after they had been awakened. Grace Coolidge suddenly realized that, in the excitement of those hours no one had thought of Miss Aurora Pierce.

Miss Pierce certainly wasn't there!

Now Mrs. Coolidge was undeniably one of the most charming ladies ever to grace the White House. This characteristic was based on her inherent, natural kindness and thoughtfulness of other people. She was a slender, handsome woman with large eyes that revealed candor and never a pretense or guile. Possibly no President's wife ever did a more noble and generous job of protecting her husband from the minor social cares and vexations than did Grace Coolidge. She was always thinking of the little things that meant so much, not necessarily to the President, but to others.

And this was one of them.

Grace Coolidge, now that her husband was ready to take the oath of office as President of the United States, turned to him and said:

"Calvin . . . Aurora isn't down. Shall I go up and wake her?"

Mr. Coolidge seemed lost in thought . . . but only for a second. He smiled slightly. For many years Aurora had done just about as she pleased in this house. She had let Calvin do only the things she thought he ought to do. She had let his father do only what she thought proper and fitting for him to do. Sometimes, he recalled in the fleeting second when the mind moves with the speed of light, she had let his father entertain guests and have them in the kitchen for a meal, but most times she hadn't. How many times, O Lord, had she refused to let the family do anything it wanted to do. He also reflected that he knew her better than anyone except his father. He knew one thing for sure: that she was still lying in bed upstairs because in that nice weighing of duty with independence, and in that grim precision by which she measured what was and what was not her business, she would never come down stairs of her own accord.

He answered his wife:

"No . . . don't wake her."

Long before her husband had become a public official, Grace Coolidge accepted his decisions without comment. She accepted this one.

She now turned to watch her husband approach the table where his father was standing with the narrow strip of paper in his hand.

She stood by him.

At this point, the very soon to be President of the United States now delayed the dramatic laden event just a second longer when he added, turning to his wife with a grin:

"Let her sleep!"

And they let her.

— END —

ACKNOWLEDGEMENTS

To all those listed on the next page I am indebted for material and counsel. With all I had interviews and from several I took tape recordings. I am especially indebted to John and Florence Coolidge, John Clement, and the distinguished Vermont author Ralph Nading Hill, all of whom went over this book in Ms. and gave me many valuable suggestions.

Interviews and correspondence were had with the following:

Calvin Coolidge
Mrs. Calvin Coolidge
Colonel John C. Coolidge
Mr. and Mrs. John Coolidge

Miss Florence Cilley	Owner of the village store
Miss Aurora Pierce	Coolidge housekeeper
Harry Ross	Secretary to President Coolidge
Mrs. W. A. Perkins	Telephone operator
Joseph McInerney	Coolidge Chauffeur
Hon. Ernest Moore	Probate Judge, Windsor County
Hon. George Jones	Probate Judge, Rutland County
Herbert Moore	Plymouth resident
Joe Moore	His son
Dallas Pollard	Cousin of Calvin Coolidge
Park Pollard	" " " "
Henry T. Brown	Senator from Windsor County
Hon. John Clement	Nephew of Governor Clement
Bessie Pratt	Coolidge Hired Girl
Howard L. Hindley	Editor Rutland Herald
Joe H. Fountain	Editor Springfield Reporter
Herbert Thompson	American Legion Commander
Leonard L. Lane	Union official
Mrs. Kate Ward	Plymouth
Ernest Carpenter	Author of book on Coolidge
Azro Johnson	Plymouth
Dr. John M. Thomas	Pres. of Norwich University
Mr. & Mrs. Charles Hoskison	Plymouth
Hon. Earle Kinsley	GOP National Committeeman from Vermont
Hon. Henry A. Wallace	Vice President
George N. Dale	Son of Congressman Dale
George C. Carter	Dun and Bradstreet
Robert A. Doray	Telephone employee

BIBLIOGRAPHY

This bibliography gives the VERBATIM *reading of the title pages of the publications listed, with the punctuation of the actual pages. Most of these volumes were first editions from my own library and constitute a comprehensive list of the books by and about President Coolidge.*

Have Faith In Massachusetts By Calvin Coolidge, Governor of Massachusetts. Boston and New York. Houghton Mifflin Company 1919. 12 mo. 224 pp. Frontis.

Calvin Coolidge His First Biography From Cornerstone to Capstone To the Accession. By R. M. Washburn. Boston. Small, Maynard and Company Publishers 1923 12mo. 150 pp. illus.

President Coolidge A Contemporary Estimate By Edward Elwell Whiting. The Atlantic Monthly Press Boston 1923 12 mo. 208 pp.

Have Faith In Calvin Coolidge Or, From a Farmhouse to The White House By Thomas T. Johnston The Christopher Publishing House Boston U. S. A. 1923 12 mo. 88 pp.

The Preparation of Calvin Coolidge An Interpretation. By Robert A. Woods. Boston and New York Houghton Mifflin Company 1924 12 mo. 284 pp.

The Price of Freedom Speeches and Addresses by Calvin Coolidge Charles Scribner's Sons New York: London 1924 12 mo. 420pp. Frontis.

Calvin Coolidge, His Ideals of Citizenship As Revealed Through His Speeches And Writings. By Edward Elwell Whiting. W. A. Wilde Company, Boston, Massachusetts 1924. 12 mo. 392 pp. Frontis.

Calvin Coolidge From a Green Mountain Farm to the White House By M. E. Hennessy. Author of "Twenty-five Years of Massachusetts Politics' "If Good Men Don't Hold Office, Bad Men Will" Calvin Coolidge. Illustrated. G. P. Putnam's Sons New York & London The Knickerbocker Press 1924 12 mo. 198 pp. Illus.

The Boyhood Days of President Calvin Coolidge or From the Green Mountains to the White House By Ernest C. Carpenter Rutland, Vermont 1925. 12 mo. 192 pp. Illus.

CALVIN COOLIDGE The Man Who Is President By William Allen White. New York The MacMillan Company 1925 12 mo. 252 pp. Illus.

THE LEGEND OF CALVIN COOLIDGE By Cameron Rogers Garden City, New York. Doubleday, Doran & Company, Inc. 1928 12 mo. 180 pp.

THE AUTOBIOGRAPHY OF CALVIN COOLIDGE New York Cosmopolitan Book Corporation 1929. 8 vo. 248 pp. Illus. Limited Edition. Numbered and signed by Calvin Coolidge.

THE RISE OF SAINT CALVIN Merry Sidelights on the Career of Mr. Coolidge. By Duff Gilfond New York The Vanguard Press 1932. 12 mo. 294 pp.

COOLIDGE WIT AND WISDOM 125 Short Stories About "Cal". Compiled by John Hiram McKee. Frederick A. Stokes Company New York 1933 small 12mo. 146 pp.

CALVIN COOLIDGE The Man From Vermont By Claude M. Fuess With Illustrations Boston Little, Brown and Company 1940. 8 vo. 522 pp. Illus.

RECOLLECTIONS OF VERMONTERS IN STATE AND NATIONAL AFFAIRS By Earle S. Kinsley, Privately Printed Rutland, Vermont 1946 T 8 vo. 170 pp. Illus.

STARLING OF THE WHITE HOUSE The Story of the man whose Secret Service detail guarded five presidents from Woodrow Wilson to Franklin D. Roosevelt as told to Thomas Sugrue by Colonel Edmund W. Starling. Simon and Shuster, New York 1946. 12 mo. 336 pp. Frontis.

HOMESPUN INAUGURAL Being An Eye-Witness Account of The Administration of The Presidential Oath of Office to Calvin Coolidge in His Father's Homestead at Plymouth, Vermont, August 3, 1923. By Joe H. Fountain, the only newspaper man present at the ceremony. 1950 St. Albans, Vermont.

GUIDE BOOK & HISTORY OF THE CALVIN COOLIDGE HOMES AT PLYMOUTH, VERMONT. Owned by the State of Vermont and Operated by The Vermont Historic Sites Commission. Written by Vrest Orton, Chairman of the Vermont Historic Sites Commission. July 1957.

SUPPLEMENT TO THE MESSAGES AND PAPERS OF THE PRESIDENTS COVERING THE SECOND ADMINISTRATION OF CALVIN COOLIDGE March 4, 1925 to March 4, 1929. With Index. Published by Bureau of National Literature (Inc) New York (no date) 8 vo. 9481 to 9850 pp. Illus.

CALVIN COOLIDGE MEMORIAL ADDRESS Delivered Before the Joint Meeting of the Two Houses of Congress as a Tribute of Respect to the Late President of the United States By Hon. Arthur Prentice Rugg, Chief Justice of the Supreme Court of Massachusetts. Hall of the House of Representatives February 6, 1933. 8 vo 77 pp. Frontis. 72nd Congress, 2d Session . . . Senate Document No. 186.

ILLUSTRATIONS

The photographs of the Coolidge Homestead and the bird's eye view of Plymouth Notch from East Mountain were taken by Geoffrey Orton, then staff photographer for the Vermont Development Commission to which I am indebted for publication permission. With the exception of two pictures used with the permission of Mrs. Charles Hoskison, all the other rare photographs hitherto unpublished in book form, are by the famous old-time New England photographer and raconteur Alton Hall Blackington, who was a newspaper and free lance photographer in Boston from the days when Coolidge was a state senator. It is to Robb Sagendorph, publisher of *Yankee Magazine*, the owner of the Blackington photographs, that I am indebted for their use here.

President Coolidge in frock and leather boots is shown talking to his father, Colonel John Coolidge, at Plymouth, on the Coolidge farm back of the Coolidge Homestead.

John Coolidge, riding in the farm wagon with his grandfather, Colonel John Coolidge. This picture was taken in June, 1925, the year before Colonel John died.

This estimate of Colonel John Coolidge, the President's father appeared in the *Guide Book of the President Coolidge Homestead*, published in 1957. In this short brochure, written by this author, and issued by the state of Vermont, I took the occasion to say that we hoped to obtain new evidence as time went on about the Coolidge story. Now the new evidence has been incorporated into this present volume.

It must be remembered that Colonel Coolidge was a remarkable example of the best type of the versatile Vermonter. He was in his lifetime a selectman, tax collector, road commissioner, school teacher, school superintendent, deputy sheriff, town constable, justice of the peace, representative in the Vermont Legislature, county senator, notary public, Dun and Bradstreet's agent, Colonel on Governor Stickney's staff and a sergeant in the Vermont National Guard. Also he was a brick and stone mason, carriage maker, a wheelwright, harness maker, undertaker, coffin maker, carpenter, tin smith, plumber, blacksmith, bookkeeper, woodsman, cattle doctor, water dowser, farmer, mechanic and store-keeper, to our knowledge. What else he may have been able to do we have no record of.

Of his father as an all-around man Calvin once said: ". . . . my father was very skillful with his hands. He had a complete set of tools, ample to do all kinds of building and carpenter work . . . . he knew how to perform all kinds of delicate operations on domestic animals. The lines he laid out were true and straight, and the curves regular. The work he did endured. If there was any physical requirement of country life which he could not perform I do not know what it was . . . ."

I don't know what finer tribute a son could pay his father than that classic sentence *"the lines he laid out were true and straight and the curves regular."*

Calvin Coolidge Says:

NORTHAMPTON, Mass., Oct. 28.—When we carefully examine it the wonder grows that, under the political practice we have developed, our government is so good.   We do not give enough attention to nominations nor elections.   We let our choice turn on some immaterial personal characteristic that has nothing to do with the qualifications for the office.   We heap so much abuse on public servants that many with every capacity for office will not subject themselves to the ordeal. Conspicuous success in private life is often considered a bar to public recognition.   In response to some whim we support candidates who can only succeed in office by disregarding the reason for which they were elected.

All of these practices put our government at a disadvantage.   We are only saved from a complete disaster because the average person rises somewhat to responsibility.   With our increasingly intricate system of government and business we must give more attention to the capacity of candidates.   Their decisions affect our whole national life.   Public service is a most exacting profession.   Honest and good intentions are almost useless unless they are supplemented by ability.   When we vote for anything but the best we cheat ourselves, our families and our country.

CALVIN COOLIDGE